THE WAY WE WERE
TEXAS

THE WAY WE WERE

TEXAS

Nostalgic Images of the Lone Star State

Wayne L. Youngblood

gpp

Guilford, Connecticut

To buy books in quantity for corporate use or incentives, call (800) 962-0973 or e-mail premiums@GlobePequot.com.

Design: Compendium design/Angela and Dave Ball
Project manager: Martin Howard
Editor: Joshua Rosenberg
Photo credits: All photographs, unless specified below, are from the Library of Congress Prints & Photographs Division—many from the Historic American Buildings Survey, Historic American Engineering Record and Historic American Landscapes Survey. Author's collection: 11T, 12T, 23T, 58B, 107B. Corbis: 18 (Radius Images), 19T (Tim Thompson), 19B (Bob Daemmrich), 20T (Tom Bean), 20B (Jeff Albertson), 21 (David Muench), 37T (Danny Lehman), 37B (Richard Cummins), 38T (Buddy Mays), 38B (Phil Schermeister), 39 (Car Culture), 55T (Charles E. Rotkin), 91 (Steven Clevenger), 97R (Bettmann), 98 (Michael Ochs Archives), 99L (Smithsonian Institution), 99R (Douglas Kirkland)

Library of Congress Cataloging-in-Publication Data

Youngblood, Wayne.
  The way we were Texas : nostalgic images of the Lone Star State / Wayne L. Youngblood.
    p. cm.
  Includes index.
  ISBN 978-0-7627-5455-7
  1. Texas--History--20th century--Pictorial works. 2. Texas--Social life and customs--20th century--Pictorial works. I. Title.

  F387.Y57 2009
  976.4'063--dc22
                                    2009025344
Printed in China

10 9 8 7 6 5 4 3 2 1

CONTENTS

INTRODUCTION

While driving across the seemingly endless central plains of Texas on a recent business trip, I remembered the impression of Texans I formed while growing up in the neighboring state of New Mexico. That image—a caricature, really—involved bigger-than-life men with ten-gallon hats and bolo ties, gum-popping women with big bouffant hairdos, and convertible Cadillac Eldorados with tops down and longhorns mounted on the hood. While my vision was admittedly exaggerated, there was some element of truth to it, as I had developed my stereotype based on the appearance of the flamboyant "Texas tourists" who came to New Mexico to hunt, fish, or take part in many of the recreational opportunities afforded by our state. But true Texans are multifaceted individuals who defy categorization.

This vision came to mind while driving the flatlands because—based on what I was seeing—it would be very easy to characterize Texas as a large expanse of flat desert with little more than tumbleweeds dotting

> *"Texas has yet to learn submission to any oppression, come from what source it may."*
>
> Sam Houston

ABOVE: Manuel Ramiriz and members of his family are shown in front of their modest home in Texas, ca. 1951. Even with post–World War II prosperity, simple homes dotted the Texas landscape.

ABOVE: Farmland in the Texas panhandle near Amarillo, Texas, ca. 1943. The plains of Texas are vast and wide open. Even a farm does little to break the beautiful but desolate landscape.

LEFT: Downtown Dallas at night in January 1942. Thriving city life in the urban areas of Texas served as stark contrast to the day-to-day lives of many rural Texans. The lure of city experience continues to draw many weekend travelers.

ABOVE: Oil gushers at Spindletop (near Beaumont) and Port Arthur (the Lucas Gusher, shown) in 1901 established Texas as an important source of petroleum, pumped money into the state, and forever changed its future.

OPPOSITE: Windmills and oil wells were two of the most common sights to break the open plains of Texas during much of the twentieth century. The Canon Ranch Eclipse Windmill in Pecos County, shown ca. 1970, is the largest functional turbine-wheel type in America.

the windy, deserted landscape. Yet this view of the Lone Star State would be no more accurate than that childhood impression I formed of her residents.

Texas is a proud and diverse country with people of all colors and lifestyles, living in every condition from abject poverty to unimaginable wealth. The landscape itself ranges from the aforementioned desert to the lush green deltas and white sandy beaches that line the Gulf of Mexico from Corpus Christi to the western border of Louisiana. Annual rainfall averages in Texas range from 5 inches to more than 60 inches! While much of the state is indeed flat, there is also the beautiful and gently rolling Hill Country surrounding Austin and the rugged Chalk and Franklin Mountain ranges near the New Mexico and Mexican borders. Elevation in the Lone Star State ranges from below sea level to 8,749 feet (Guadalupe Peak).

Start anywhere in Texas and drive for a few hours, and the area you end up in will look completely different from the area where you started. Texas has flat desert, barrier islands, hilly grasslands, soggy swamps, dense forests, sandy beaches, windy plateaus, and, with man's

presence, forms of habitation ranging from ghost towns and small villages to the urban centers of Dallas, Fort Worth, San Antonio, and Houston.

Indeed, Texas features topographical, weather, and geographical elements of the South, Southwest, Great Plains, Rocky Mountains, and the Gulf, and the flora and fauna to match. This diversity is due at least in part to the state's sheer size. Because it is so large, Texas is generally divided into four major geographical regions, including the Gulf Coastal Plains, Great Plains, Interior Lowlands, and the Basin and Range Province, each with its own characteristics (and, of course, overlaps).

With about 268,600 square miles, the state of Texas is second in size only to Alaska, and includes about 7 percent of the entire area of the United States. A rather fun exercise is to try to figure out how many states could fit inside the borders of Texas. To pick on our nation's smallest state—Rhode Island (1,545 square miles)—one could fit almost 174 Rhode Islands in Texas. Or, to look at it another way, the entire states of Illinois (57,918 square miles), Missouri (69,709 square miles), Pennsylvania

RIGHT: Although inactive since 1905, the Port Isabel Lighthouse (built in 1853 and shown here in 1942) is familiar to most Texans. It is one of five surviving lighthouses located along the Gulf of Mexico.

BELOW: After spring runoff, many rivers and streams of the Southwest are dry, as shown by these wagon tracks along the Colorado River in May 1939. Fast and severe thunderstorms can turn dry riverbeds and arroyos into deep and roiling rivers within minutes.

(46,058 square miles), New Jersey (8,722 square miles), New York (54,475 square miles), West Virginia (24,231 square miles), and Connecticut (5,544 square miles) could fit, with 1,943 square miles (Rhode Island–plus) left over!

The diversity found in Texas goes way beyond flora and fauna or geographical and financial differences. The state's history is varied as well—to the point that there have been six flags over Texas, including those of Spain, France, Mexico,

TOP RIGHT: The state flower of Texas since 1901, the bluebonnet is so named for the petal structure, which resembles a woman's sunbonnet. The early spring flowers are found throughout central and south Texas in fields and along roadsides.

RIGHT: Rising over the Texas horizon like a major thunderstorm, the intense black clouds in this March 1936 photo are composed of dust. Survivors of Dust Bowl storms described the sand penetrating every nook and cranny in their homes.

ABOVE: Small streams such as this one photographed in Austin—and the resulting vegetation that grows along them—provide shady and cool oases for humans and animals alike, as well as a very welcoming appearance.

the Republic of Texas, the Confederate States of America, and the United States.

The first white men to explore what is now Texas were the Spanish Conquistadores, who encountered the Hasinai people (a confederation of several Caddo-speaking tribes of American Indians) during the sixteenth century. The Hasinai referred to "Tejas" or "taysha," loosely translated as "friend" or "ally." The Spanish, who initially had a great deal of respect for the Hasinai, came to refer to them as "the great kingdom of Tejas." The name stuck.

In 1519, only twenty-seven years after Columbus first visited the New World, Captain Alonso de Pineda reached the area eventually called Texas, accessing it through the Gulf of Mexico. In 1528, a shipwrecked Cabeza de Vaca became the first European to walk across Texas. He later published a journal giving descriptions of the flora, fauna, and natives encountered.

LEFT: A common sight during the late nineteenth and early twentieth centuries was the hardworking cowboy. In this 1907 image a cowboy sits on horseback atop a knoll, looking down at a herd of cattle on the LS Ranch range.

LEFT: A group of three Texas cowboys relaxes for their afternoon meal under a tree on the LS Ranch in 1907. They are eating tomatoes from a can.

In 1685, the French attempted to begin colonizing parts of Texas (near present-day Louisiana), but failed. After an 1821 revolution led by Agustin de Iturbide, Mexico (which included Texas) declared her independence from Spain. Soon, thousands of colonists, led by Stephen F. Austin, settled in the new areas. During the next fifteen years the population of colonists mushroomed. These folks included former traders, frontiersman, and others. By 1836, foreigners outnumbered the Mexican population of Texas five-to-one (25,000 to 5,000). In 1830, Mexico halted immigration and combined Texas with the state of Coahuila (its capital in Saltillo was more than 600 miles from northeastern Texas). In 1833 Antonio Lopez de Santa Anna (originally a soldier with the Spanish army) officially became president of Mexico, then its self-proclaimed dictator. He abolished the 1824 constitution and began centralizing his government.

On October 2, 1835, the Texas Revolution began with the first shot fired at Gonzales. The revolution continued with the bloody battle of The Alamo (February 23 to March 6, 1836), the gal-

vanizing event of the conflict. Spurred on by cries of "Remember The Alamo," Texans threw off the Mexican yoke soon after at the Battle of San Jacinto (April 21, 1836), although the Republic of Texas (a sovereign state) had been declared on March 2, 1836, during the bloodshed at The Alamo. The Mexicans refused to acknowledge the republic and there were other attacks.

Nine years later, on December 29, 1845, President James K. Polk signed legislation making Texas the twenty-eighth state of the Union. Statehood did not, however, magically solve the many problems that plagued Texans, including Indian raids and hostility with Mexico. American expansionist policies pushed Mexico further, leading to the Mexican-American War in 1846. The war was concluded with the Treaty of Guadalupe-Hidalgo in 1848.

Almost from the beginning, Texans relied heavily on black slave labor for their cotton crops and other needs. In 1860 an estimated 30 percent of the state's population was slaves. It's no surprise that as the Civil War heated up, Texas sided with the Confederate States of America (CSA). On February 1, 1861,

LEFT: In Texas, getting water to where it is needed is vital. Elaborate aqueducts, such as the Piedras Creek Aqueduct, shown ca. 1968, help.

ABOVE: Once oil was discovered in Texas (and the demand for its use in combustible-fuel engines grew), so did oil boom towns, such as this one near the Red River. Oil derricks sometimes outnumbered residents in these communities.

BELOW: Cowboys on the XIT Ranch in 1904 gather and brand cattle. Each ranch had a unique brand pattern to identify free-range cattle. Even branding did not stop cattle theft, however.

ABOVE: Texas boasts a number of interesting surviving rural structures. This brick residence of the owner of the brick works in Medina County was built in 1913.

Texas officially seceded from the Union, becoming a part of the CSA.

Texans are very strongly associated with cowboys and ranching—a stereotype founded on fact, as farming and ranching have always been a strong part of the economy of the state. After the Civil War, Texas began ranching in earnest, raising primarily longhorn cattle. The relative wealth of Texans grew steadily for most of the rest of the nineteenth century, remaining fairly strong even when the national economy was doing poorly.

Just barely into the twentieth century, everything changed once again for Texas. On January 10, 1901, the eruption of the Lucas Gusher at Spindletop (near the southeast corner of Texas) culminated a several-year search for oil in the area. The gusher shot more than 150 feet in the air at a rate of nearly 100,000 barrels of oil per day. Things have never been the same.

Oil towns soon began to spring up all over Texas, with derricks often outnumbering buildings. Oil-generated wealth led to a lifestyle for many Texans far beyond the reach of most Americans. Arguably, the two substances most important to Texas are water and oil, so it's no surprise that, historically, two of the most common

structures found were windmills and oil derricks. Of course now, with decreased oil production and modern plumbing, both are less commonly seen than they used to be, but they are still found all over the state—both active and inactive.

The Dust Bowl years of the 1930s were very tough for Texans; the economy was poor, and the weather was worse. The term "Dust Bowl" was coined after the "Black Sunday" storm of April 14, 1935, when a black cloud of dust obscured much of the Midwest. During this time tens of thousands of Texans were out of work and many lost their homes. One would not expect these times of hard-scrabble life and deep poverty to spawn nostalgic feelings. But oddly, if you visit with most any old-timer who survived the Dust Bowl years, you'll find some very deep and strong feelings for simpler times. Farmers' markets and other small-town businesses were the epitome of the can-do attitude that allowed the state to recover from the Dust Bowl era.

And recover it did! Today, people are pouring into Texas almost faster than the state can absorb them. Since 2000, the population of Texas has grown by nearly 13 percent, more than double that of the

ABOVE: The Caddo Indians of Texas were among the southern and Midwestern groups of mound builders. The Davis mound site, near Alto, is considered one of the most significant.

OPPOSITE: El Capitan takes on a luminous appearance in the background of this image, with prickly pear and other cactus in the foreground. The Guadalupe range is known for its beauty.

RIGHT: The sand along South Padre Island (the longest barrier island in the world) is among the whitest found in the state. Here, a dune with grasses and morning primrose juts up from the beach.

national average, and tops out at more than twenty-four million.

This book takes a fond look back at the relatively recent past of the state of Texas. Some of the images involve things experienced uniquely by Texans, while others are universal reflections of the human condition. Still other photos will evoke feelings of times and places gone for good. Many of these snippets of Texas life are guaranteed to bring a smile. Y'all pull up a chair, sit back, and relax with *The Way We Were: Texas*.

OPPOSITE, TOP: A hiker is silhouetted in shadow against the deep blue sky as he climbs volcanic rock outcroppings near Burro Mesa (right) in Big Bend National Park.

OPPOSITE, BOTTOM: Nudie Cohn (1902–1984), rodeo tailor and western tailor to the stars, exemplified the flamboyant image of rhinestone-studded Texans. He was not a native Texan (born in the Ukraine), but he was closely associated with the Lone Star State.

RIGHT: Of all the sights in Big Bend National Park, Santa Elena Canyon is considered perhaps the most spectacular. The canyon, with sheer cliffs, was cut over the centuries by the Rio Grande River.

MAJOR ATTRACTIONS

Whether you are boating or hiking through beautiful Big Bend National Park, hiking the Guadalupe Mountains, or doing both at the Aransas National Wildlife Refuge, you are enjoying Texas at its finest. Or, if you prefer studying the graffiti-covered, half-buried car bodies at Cadillac Ranch, riding the Titan or Texas Giant at Six Flags Over Texas amusement park, or taking in the sights at the National Cowgirl Museum & Hall of Fame, you're still seeing Texas at its best. You can divide major attractions in Texas into two essential groups: natural and man-made, each of which showcases different facets of the depth and breadth of the Lone Star State. Due at least in part to its sheer size,

ABOVE: A number of county courthouses throughout the state show a great deal of character, but the still-inhabited Bexar County Courthouse in San Antonio is among the most popular as a destination.

LEFT: The architectural design of the Texas State Capitol, built from 1882 to 1886, was the result of a national contest to replace the structure that burned in 1881. The building is a true showpiece.

LEFT: The Mission Señora de la Purísima Concepción. The Spanish colonial period of Texas is filled with huge and elaborate missions and their tales. At one time more than forty missions existed (more than in California).

virtually anything can be found in Texas, ranging from the sublime to the ridiculous.

Among the most significant attractions of either category to Texans, however, is The Alamo, located in downtown San Antonio where it is dwarfed by surrounding skyscrapers. This piece of living history is easily the most recognizable landmark to non-Texans as well.

The Alamo has a turbulent history and never served its original purpose. Built in 1744 from locally mined limestone, the structure was intended to be the church for the Mission San Antonio

ABOVE: San Juan Capistrano Mission was originally founded in East Texas in 1716, but was transferred to its present site in 1756. A larger church was started, but never completed, the foundation of which is still visible. Maintenance and guiding of visitors is done by the National Park Service.

de Valero (founded in 1718 to convert Indians to Christianity), although it was never completed as planned. It was, however, successfully used as a church until 1793, after which it was abandoned.

Soon the building (and the rest of the compound), not yet known by its current name, was used to garrison Spanish soldiers, and it even served as San Antonio's first hospital from 1806 to 1812. In 1821, The Alamo was transferred from Spanish to Mexican control and continued to be used by soldiers until December 1835, when it was taken over by Texans during the Texas Revolution. Texans held it through the Battle of The Alamo, February 23 to March 6, 1836, when all remaining defenders were killed. The Mexicans held the complex for several months, until they lost the revolution. As the Mexicans withdrew, they destroyed much of the complex and set fires throughout. In 1840, the San Antonio town council passed a resolution that allowed local residents to remove stone from The Alamo for personal use at the rate of $5 per wagonload.

But the looted and badly beaten-up

RIGHT: Established about 1740, Mission San José y San Miguel de Aguayo (shown in 1936) is the most complete of the remaining eighteenth-century mission complexes in San Antonio. The surviving buildings are of significance to Texas colonial history and provide the contemporary observer with a strong visual concept of the frontier institution.

RIGHT: Ramparts were an important part of the San José Mission. Their sole purpose was to protect inhabitants against attacks by hostile Indians. All eighteenth-century Spanish missions included ramparts in building plans.

Alamo's military history was not yet over. U.S. Army soldiers appropriated part of the complex for use by the quartermaster during the 1846 Mexican-American War, and it was taken over by the Confederate Army during the Civil War. After the U.S. Army took possession of The Alamo after the war, the Catholic Church requested that the army leave the facility so it could be used as a place of worship by local German Catholics. The army refused but ultimately abandoned The Alamo in 1876. The convent (where most of the Alamo defenders were killed) was sold

ABOVE: The Dallas City Hall is notable for several architectural reasons such as the sloped angle of the building, but also is well known for its large Henry Moore sculpture.

and used as a wholesale grocery business. Little thought was given to the building's historical significance.

After much debate over the future of The Alamo (including the possibility of razing it), state representative Samuel Ealy Johnson, Jr. (father of future president Lyndon Baines Johnson) sponsored a bill in 1905 that, among other things, named the Daughters of the Republic of Texas custodian of the chapel and convent. Due to bickering and financial problems, relatively little was done to preserve The Alamo until after it was designated a National Historic Landmark in 1960. The convent (long barracks) was roofed and converted to a museum in preparation for HemisFair, the World's Fair that was held in San Antonio in 1968. The Alamo now

ABOVE: The Lee County Courthouse, located deep in the heart of Texas (about 55 miles east of Austin), was completed in 1899. It was one of the last designed by James Riley Gordon, who was responsible for a number of characteristic Texas courthouses.

LEFT: Designated a National Historic Landmark in 1986, the Texas State Capitol is the fourth building in Austin to house the government of the state. It is the largest state capitol in terms of square footage and second in total size only to the National Capitol in D.C.

BELOW: Throughout the Texas State Capitol, in hallways and in nooks, there are sculptures of notable Texans and other historical figures.

attracts more than four million visitors each year, making it among the most popular of all U.S. historic sites.

Related to The Alamo are numerous Spanish missions—at one time supposedly more than forty (a higher number than in California). Most of these missions were established during the 1700s to convert Indians to Christianity. The plan was not to colonize Texas with Spaniards and displace the Indians, but rather to turn the natives into loyal God-fearing taxpayers. Despite the grand nature of some missions, few had any lasting success and virtually all were abandoned by the time Mexico achieved her independence from Spain in 1821. Although most missions that still have a physical presence are little more than ruins, several buildings survive relatively intact and are popular attractions.

Another interesting and important man-made attraction is the Texas State Capitol in Austin, an Italian Renaissance Revival–style structure built from 1882 to 1886. This building was the result of a national contest to design a new capitol to replace one destroyed by fire in 1881. The winning design was based on the Capitol in Washington, D.C. At 360,000 square feet,

Texas's building is the largest state capitol in the United States. The capitol features portraits of every individual who served as president of the Republic of Texas or as governor of the state, as well as sculptures of Sam Houston, Stephen Austin, and many others. The acoustics of the rotunda make it an effective whispering hall.

Hemisfair Park in San Antonio is what remains of the 1968 World's Fair, which commemorated the 250th anniversary of the founding of the city. During the six months of the fair, more than six and a half million visitors came from all over the world. The most recognizable structure of the grounds, The Tower of the Americas, is still quite popular.

The mother of all highways, as historic Route 66 is known, passes nearly straight across the Texas panhandle, a relatively short distance of 180 miles within the state. But during its heyday that distance (the second lowest of any state through which the highway passes)

was loaded with roadside attractions ranging from restaurants to gimmicks. Included among these were Route 66 Midpoint (at Adrian, Texas), Cadillac Ranch (and its copycat Bug Ranch), Cowboy Motel, and Leaning Water Tower, to name a few.

Down south, in Houston, is the

BELOW: L.R. Timlin designed this ornate Spanish Baroque architectural detail on the San Antonio structure built in 1931 for Southwest Bell Telephone. The building is located in the Monte Vista National Historic District.

OPPOSITE: Crystal City is considered the "spinach capital of the world." This monument to Popeye, who derives his strength from spinach, was erected in 1937, the year after the town's first Spinach Festival.

Lyndon B. Johnson Space Center, opened in 1963. The center houses Mission Control Center, the heartbeat of the NASA Space Program, where all flights are monitored and astronauts trained. Old spacecraft (including vehicles used in the Mercury, Gemini, and Apollo programs) can be found on the grounds, and a fascinating visitor complex guides guests through the history of the U.S. space program.

Other major attractions in the state include the Padre Island National Seashore (near Corpus Christi), the Caddoan Mounds State Historic Site (near Nacogdoches), the Lady Bird Johnson Wildflower Center (near Austin), the Texas Sports Hall of Fame (in Waco), the Buddy Holly Center (in Lubbock), the American Quarter Horse Heritage Center & Museum (in Amarillo), and even the Neiman Marcus department store in Dallas, which was established there in 1907. The store's claim to fame is that one can find anything from a spool of thread to a mummy in a case there. There are hundreds of other attractions throughout the state, including some that are known to few other than locals.

LEFT: Mission San Francisco de la Espada was founded as San Francisco de los Tejas in East Texas in 1690, making it the first mission in the state. It did not prosper, however, and was moved to the present site in 1731 and completed in 1756.

BELOW, FAR LEFT: The front doorway of Mission San Francisco de la Espada is particularly notable because of its multifoil arch.

BELOW, LEFT: As San Antonio grew rapidly during the early decades of the twentieth century, the city began to engulf The Alamo. The building at left dwarfs the monument in 1926. This was just the beginning.

OPPOSITE: This house was once inhabited by "Seminole-Negros," descendants of escaped slaves who settled in Florida, mixing with the Seminole Indians. They were excellent scouts for the army during the 1870s.

ABOVE: The Hotel Galvez, named for Bernardo de Galvez, namesake of Galveston, was newly constructed when this image was taken in 1911. The hotel was long known as the "Queen of the Gulf." It is now part of the Wyndham chain.

ABOVE: The Saturn V rocket at NASA's Johnson Space Center in Houston is just one of the many spacecraft on display.

MILLION DOLLAR
HOTEL GALVEZ
ON SEAWALL BOULEVARD
GALVESTON, TEXAS.

ABOVE: As the heart of NASA, the Johnson Space Center in Houston is a mecca for anyone interested in space travel. Visitors can see historic artifacts or operate simulators.

LEFT: The Rattler is one of the many roller coasters and other rides found at the three different Six Flags Over Texas amusement parks in Fiesta, Arlington, and Houston, Texas. The parks have drawn millions of visitors.

OPPOSITE: The Tower Service Station of Shamrock lies on the "Crossroads of America," so named because of the intersection of two major highways, Route 66 and Route 83. Local ranchers built the imposing structure in 1936 to attract attention.

LEFT: Although still given its own space, The Alamo, in downtown San Antonio, is nearly completely surrounded by skyscrapers and other urban structures, making it seem rather anachronistic with its surroundings.

TRANSPORTATION

Although the history of transportation in Texas in the latter half of the twentieth century essentially mirrors that of much of the rest of the United States, earlier transportation was dominated primarily by the horse and railroad, both of which eventually gave way in large part to the automobile.

Unlike most other parts of the country, including much of the East Coast, small Texas towns are separated by vast distances. As a result, communities were quite isolated and self-supporting during much of the nineteenth and early twentieth centuries. Distances were measured not as much by miles as by how many days on horseback, and many Texans lived their entire lives without ever having left the state or, in some cases, even their own county.

Prior to the 1850s, when the Texas Territory still included half of what is now New Mexico and a slice of Colorado, most "settled land" was along the river bottoms of south and eastern Texas, and along the Gulf Coast. Steamboats plied the waters of the lower Rio Grande, Trinity, and Brazos

> *"I feel safer on a racetrack than I do on Houston's freeways."*
>
> A. J. Foyt, USAC's all-time career wins record holder

ABOVE: The Kingdom Stone Arch Bridge, the longest masonry arch bridge in Texas, was created by the Works Progress Administration (WPA) during the early 1940s. The bridge, with eighteen stone arches, is located on the Brazos River, a mile below Morris Sheppard Dam.

ABOVE: Rainbow Bridge, ca. 1980, spans the Neches River, linking Beaumont with the Gulf of Mexico. Construction began in 1938 on what became the tallest bridge in the southern United States and one of the tallest in the world when completed. It has a vertical clearance of 176 feet and a length of 7,752 feet, needed to allow the passage of ocean-going cargo ships and tankers. The bridge's construction required innovative engineering methods, both because of its height and because it had to be built to withstand hurricane-force (up to 150 mph) winds.

ABOVE: The Main Street Viaduct in Fort Worth was the first concrete arch bridge in the United States to employ self-supporting reinforcing steel. Old and new city structures contrast with each other in the background.

Rivers, but year-round transportation was not really possible because the rivers became too shallow during the summer months. The few roads that existed (used primarily by oxcarts, wagons, and stagecoaches) were rough at best and impossible to use during wet weather that turned them into clay pits.

Horses were the first vital means of reliable transportation for early Texans. Although it is generally accepted that horses as we know them evolved in North America and eventually migrated to Europe across the Bering Strait, they weren't plentiful here until the Spaniards began bringing them into the area during the seventeenth and eighteenth centuries. The highly adaptable species began to breed in the wilderness of North America. By the time Anglo settlers began establishing towns throughout what is now Texas, there were huge herds of wild mustangs from which sturdy horses could be captured and trained. To the rancher the horse was a trusted vehicle, tool, friend, partner, and—occasionally—confidante. Horses are still very important to rural Texans for farm and ranch chores, although their days of long journeys across the vast state are generally over. Still, it's

ABOVE: The Pecos River Gorge is the location of two very high bridges: the 1892 Pecos Viaduct and the current structure (shown), its 1944 successor. Increased traffic during World War II necessitated replacement of this critical link on a major east-west railroad.

not unusual in smaller towns to see horses ambling through the streets fairly regularly and, as recently as the 1930s and 1940s, horses could be seen in large numbers, tied alongside parked automobiles at farm markets and downtown events.

By the latter part of the nineteenth century, much of the United States was connected by the railroad system. As various routes spidered out across the land, Americans had access to people and places they could previously only have dreamed about. In Texas, transportation by rail was a godsend, but its expansion into the state was slow and came with challenges, including crossing Indian-owned land in Oklahoma. Canals, river improvements, plank roads, and other means of transportation had been tried, but ultimately viability depended upon the rails.

The Texas Rail Road, Navigation and Banking Company was formed December 16, 1836, but, because of internal corruption and other problems, no rails were ever constructed. Other railroad schemes were attempted, but none materialized until late 1852, when the first locomotive was delivered to run a 20-mile segment that opened in 1853. By 1861, nine railroad companies existed in Texas, but fewer than

ABOVE: Will Harris is shown in 1924 with his family and his inventive "auto house," built on a truck chassis. This early version of a motorized camping trailer allowed for great freedom.

BELOW: This Texas Oil Company (later Texaco) service station ca. 1925 features very careful landscaping, a well-decorated building, and neatly placed pumps and signage, all signs of pride and customer service.

LEFT: In the 1920s a delivery driver stands by a Texaco gas truck that bears the notation, "TEX Petroleum, Made by the Texas." The truck also is carrying Thuban Compound (to cover gear teeth) and Motor Cup Grease.

ABOVE: The corner service station was frequently a gathering spot for locals. The James Burke Station (shown in 1925) benefited from its location near a loan office and hot dog stand. Note the billboards in the background.

500 miles of track had been laid. The Missouri-Kansas-Texas Railway Company brought real growth. Incorporated May 23, 1870, the company was the first to enter Texas from the north, in 1872, and finally connected Texas with the rest of the country's railway system. Because the stock exchange symbol for the railroad was K-T, it soon became known fondly as the "Katy." By the turn of the century, there were still fewer than 10,000 miles of track (less than 5 percent of the country's total), but things were moving fast, and by 1911 Texas had more miles of track than any other state—a claim it can still make.

Within a few years of the invention of the automobile, Texans developed a love affair with driving for both leisure and work, much like the rest of the country. Service stations, travel bureaus, drive-ins, and tourist traps began springing up along the way. Automobiles and pickups were pressed into service to get products to market, and service stations soon overshadowed blacksmith shops—many providing their own peculiar style.

As the twentieth century went on, the transportation infrastructure of Texas grew to include roads, rails, bridges, airports, and more. A person could now drive, ride a bus or train, or even fly to remote destinations in the state within a few hours—journeys that would have taken many days not so many years earlier.

OPPOSITE: Throughout Texas auto travel bureaus in main towns acted as brokers for passengers and drivers wanting to share the expense of traveling the long distances between Texas towns.

LEFT: With the popularity of the automobile and cheap, readily available gasoline, auto travel bureaus (the forerunners of today's travel agents) such as this one in Harlingen began to pop up as a form of service.

LEFT: Just as motorists had to stop in at service stations to check their oil and tires, those who rode horses had to make regular trips to the blacksmith to have their horseshoes checked. This San Antonio shop is shown in 1939.

RIGHT: In many rural areas of Texas, horses were still about as common as automobiles in downtown areas as late as the 1960s. This horse was being displayed and sold in Alpine in 1939.

RIGHT: A group of farmers visit at market in downtown Weatherford in 1939. The presence of both horses and cars was common.

LEFT: Even by 1939, when this image was taken of the Farmers' Supply Store, the horse and wagon was still the preferred form of transportation for many farmers and ranchers.

LEFT: When automobiles were used by farmers for taking merchandise to market, produce and small livestock were loaded in the back and often displayed on the hood or running board.

OPPOSITE: Small stations throughout rural America, such as this one in San Marcos, stocked used tires for those who had problems on the road. This not only eliminated waste of limited resources, but provided a useful service. The level of wear determined price.

ABOVE: A conductor reads his orders near the train on the Atchison, Topeka, and Santa Fe Railroad between Amarillo, Texas, and Clovis, New Mexico, in 1943. Such trains were vital links for Texans living in remote villages.

RIGHT: A man waves from the caboose as his train passes an eastbound freight train on the Atchison, Topeka, and Santa Fe Railroad between Amarillo, Texas, and Clovis, New Mexico, in 1943.

ABOVE: Railroad yardmasters coordinate traffic and worker activities, including making and breaking trains and yard switching. They also review train schedules and switching orders. Note the maps and extensive paperwork.

LEFT: Freight cars, water cars, boxcars, and many others wait in the extensive railroad yards of Amarillo for their next journey in 1942. Although the locomotive arrived in Texas late compared to other areas, it became the lifeblood of transportation.

LEFT: The locomotive *Sabine* of Morgan's Louisiana & Texas line, ca. 1909–1932. Although this locomotive had served its useful time by the time the photo was taken, it is representative of late nineteenth century locomotives in Texas.

LEFT: The *Prosperity Special* crossing the Pecos River, near Langtry, Texas, ca. 1922. The Pecos River Viaduct spanned 2,180 feet, 321 feet above the river. For years, the metal structure was the highest bridge in the United States and the third highest in the world. Note the number of engines on the train.

RIGHT: Superseded by the Dallas-Fort Worth International Airport in 1973, Love Field was Dallas' main airport in 1967 when this photograph was taken. Four years earlier, Lyndon B. Johnson had been sworn in as president on Air Force One at Love Field following the assassination of John F. Kennedy.

RIGHT: A 1939 image of the Airport Administration Building in Fort Worth shows the care put into forms of transportation thought to be vital to the state. The building is one of several notable airports in Texas.

LEISURE ACTIVITIES

In part due to the sheer size and scope of the landscape of Texas, residents have absolutely no trouble finding fun and interesting things to do, whether it is taking in the wonders of nature, enjoying man-made amusements such as the Six Flags Over Texas amusement parks, or participating in countless other pleasurable diversions from sandlot baseball to professional sports.

Parades, pageants, pick-up baseball games, carnivals (with their rides and sideshows), games of jump rope or Cowboys and Indians, and going to the movies are all traditional forms of entertainment that have been enjoyed for decades by Texans. But there are other leisure activities that seem to take on a life of their own in the Lone Star State.

With the state's heavy agricultural influence, it's no surprise food is a very large part of the leisure life of Texans. In farmers' markets and on street corners all over the state, there are small vendors of all types of food, ranging from carnitas to

ABOVE: Conceived as home of the Houston Colts (later Astros) and Houston Oilers, the Astrodome, termed by some as the "Eighth Wonder of the World," was completed in 1964. It marked the first time a fully enclosed stadium was built for both baseball and football.

ABOVE: The Astrodome, originally called Harris County Domed Stadium, covers 9.14 acres of land and is circular in shape. The outer diameter of the Astrodome is 710 feet, and the clear span of the dome roof is 642 feet.

ABOVE: A number of Texas cities have begun incorporating attractive walkways with historical structures, such as the Augusta Street Bridge, which spans the San Antonio River.

ABOVE: Craft fairs and art festivals, such as this one near downtown Austin, have long been a mainstay to those looking for pleasant diversions in the city.

Cajun, from barbecued brisket to baba ghanoush. Hundreds of tiny diners and restaurants dot the landscape of small towns and big cities, and the state has plenty of five-star restaurants to boot. But the three most well-known and beloved foods of Texans, and of those who visit, are Mexican (including the Tex-Mex variant), Cajun, and barbecue. Some folks are even willing to drive scores of miles to get a fix of their favorite barbecue, bowl of chili, or boudin sausage. The unofficial state dish, however, is still chicken-fried steak (which originated in Texas), and this breaded, tenderized fried cube steak can be found slathered in peppered milk gravy throughout the state.

But Texans do more than eat. Music is deeply woven into the fabric of the state's heritage. Beginning with the Indians, then the first European settlers, people have been making and enjoying music on the prairie for many years, in their living rooms and front porches, at family celebrations, and more recently at nightclubs and even larger venues.

Drawing on the influences of Anglo, Mexican, German, and other cultures, various forms of music evolved in the state using stringed instruments, brass, and

ABOVE: Miss Jovita Gonzalez and several students give an outdoor radio performance under a tree on the grounds of St. Mary's Academy in San Antonio in 1934.

even the accordion. Mariachi bands, blasting their trumpet-guitar-accordion–based music, can be found everywhere, playing flashy music with strong beats that are very much like the polka. For all practical purposes country music as we know it developed in Texas, with the help of Texans Bob Wills, Waylon Jennings, and Willie Nelson, to name a few. Blues, too, grew legs in Texas, inspired by the music of Blind Lemon Jefferson.

The accepted hub of the Texas music scene is Austin, where acts from small bands working for drinks and tips to well-known national performers can be found—sometimes in the same place! The city's annual South by Southwest (SXSW) event, held for nearly twenty-five years, draws tens of thousands of music lovers from all over the world, and has become one of the most influential music events in the country.

In sports, Texas boasts two professional football teams (Dallas Cowboys and Houston Texans), three professional basketball teams (Dallas Mavericks, San Antonio Spurs, and Houston Rockets), two professional baseball teams (Houston Astros and Texas Rangers), one professional hockey team (Dallas Stars), and

two professional soccer teams (FC Dallas and Houston Dynamo). In women's sports the San Antonio Silver Spurs compete in the Women's National Basketball Association. In addition, there are dozens of athletes who are engaged professionally in every sport from bowling to bicycling.

College sports are also followed avidly all over the state. Athletic teams are fielded by Angelo State, Baylor University, Midland College, Rice University, Southern Methodist University, Texas A&M, Texas Tech, University of Texas (all locations), and dozens of other colleges and universities. These compete in football, basketball, baseball, soccer, wrestling, volleyball, swimming, tennis, track, and more, and frequently win national championships. Texans take their sports (professional and college) seriously!

Fairs and festivals also are popular in Texas. In addition to the state fair and

ABOVE: Regardless of whether it's a break from the day's chores or a day-long outing, many rural Texans (such as this couple shown in 1937) enjoy horseback riding for fun.

RIGHT: A pair of young girls dance and play in their backyard, as neighbor boys watch from the street through a fence (ca. 1934).

ABOVE: With six-shooters loaded with caps, this group of boys (some barefoot) plays the ever-present game of Cowboys and Indians in 1942 in a Farm Services Administration camp.

county fairs in each of Texas's 254 counties, there are scores of other festivals and celebrations that mark everything from Juneteenth and Cinco de Mayo to Oysterfest (Fulton) and Black-eyed Pea Jamboree (Athens).

No discussion of Texas leisure activities would be complete without mentioning rodeo, which is practiced and watched by millions of Texans and helps keep the flavor of the Old West alive. Rodeos are not unique to Texas, but with their emphasis on horses and livestock, these events have always been a large part of Texas rural life. The grandstands are still packed at most places during rodeo season, which now encompasses much of the year. Related events, such as barbecue and chili cookoffs, bandstand performances, carnivals, various competitions of skill and athletic prowess, and the crowning of the rodeo queen all serve to reinforce the importance of rodeo to those living "out west" in Texas.

OPPOSITE: A San Augustine grade school in 1939. Recess provided a welcome break for kids to head out to the playground from the classroom, choose sides, and play a pick-up game of baseball.

LEFT: One of the most common forms of entertainment from the 1940s through the 1970s was going to traveling carnivals and midways. These rides frequently set up on vacant ground in small towns, such as this carnival in Brownsville in 1942.

LEFT: The interior of a small hamburger stand in 1939 (with waitress and cook waiting for customers) shows well-worn and mismatched seats and counter. The menu was simple and the food was comfortable.

BELOW: In 1940 spectators wait in line to enter the grandstand for a rodeo connected with a stock show in San Angelo. The young boy near the lower right is dressed in his finest cowboy outfit.

RIGHT: Rodeos were not only big entertainment, but big business throughout Texas. Note the spectators lined up on the fence.

BELOW: A young woman rodeo performer waits atop her horse to enter the grandstand in 1940. This entertainer has a bucking bronco embroidered on her blouse.

BELOW, RIGHT: Horse tricks were every bit as popular as bull or bronco riding at rodeos. Here a nattily dressed trainer is kissed by his horse.

ABOVE: As spectators watch with delight from the fence, a bull chases two men around the ring at the San Angelo Fat Stock Show in 1940. An insurance ad is painted on the fence.

LEFT: Revelers in costumes, military uniforms, and dresses dance during the Charro Days Fiesta at the El Rancho Grande in 1942.

ABOVE, LEFT: A young man tunes his guitar before playing at a Farm Security Administration camp in Weslaco in 1942. Folk music was a large part of everyday life.

ABOVE: A member of the Mexican orchestra at the El Rancho Grande plays his violin at the Brownsville Charro Days celebration. The trumpeter in the background suggests this was likely mariachi-style music.

LEFT: Family music was a very important form of Texas entertainment. It not only honed talents, but took minds off problems. A brother and sister play banjo and guitar for their younger siblings in 1942.

LEFT: A sign at a Corpus Christi trailer court ca. 1940 shows various amusements planned for the residents, including shuffleboard, cards, dominos, checkers, and chess. Such diversions provided important socialization.

ABOVE: A Hidalgo County couple relaxes at home in 1939, reading and sewing as they listen to the radio. The radio was the center of attention in many homes.

OPPOSITE: Parades in small towns celebrate everything from Independence Day to local historical events. It's not unusual to see as many participants as spectators.

Copyright 1912

ABOVE: Pageants, such as this First International Pageant of Pulchritude
& Seventh Annual Bathing Girl Revue held in 1926 in Galveston, gave
residents the opportunity to blow off steam. Here, contestants from
Flint to San Antonio are dressed in their bathing finest.

BELOW: These women, competing in the 1923 Bathing Girl Revue, are dressed in everything from simple bathing suits to elaborate reproductions of Egyptian costuming.

LEFT: A peanut salesman hawks his product in a 1940 rodeo grandstand, as the San Angelo High School Band plays. Note the man's makeshift peanut box and lumberyard apron.

RIGHT: Ticket sellers and barkers served a very important function at fair midways and traveling carnivals. They helped guide and direct the crowds and added to the experience.

BUSINESS AND INSTITUTIONS

While there are many types of businesses that operate throughout Texas (including multinational corporations in the large cities), the Lone Star State has been dominated by agriculture and oil. Whether it's citrus fruit, livestock, cotton, or a host of additional small cash crops, the state has relied on the resources of the earth for its prosperity. And prosper it has. If Texas was once again on its own as an independent republic, its economy would be the tenth largest in the world.

Small towns still have bakeries, boot shops, saddleries, and other businesses, and farmers' markets are no small matter in many towns and cities. But much focus is still placed on the behemoths of Texas business.

Livestock production (particularly cattle) is a huge part of Texas's identity and its economy. There are thousands of ranches of all sizes, some huge. The King Ranch (located near Kingsville, Texas, in the south), at 825,000 acres across four counties, is larger than the land mass of

> *"Texas can make it without the United States, but the United States can't make it without Texas."*
>
> Governor Sam Houston

ABOVE: The Lundberg Bakery was in operation until 1937. Located within a block of both the Texas State Capitol and the Governor's Mansion, the restored Victorian structure makes a significant visual contribution to the Capitol Area.

ABOVE: The Lundberg Bakery is an important commercial and historical landmark in Austin. Built in 1875 and 1876, it housed the first successful bakery business of Charles Lundberg. Shown is the baking area in the late 1960s, looking east.

BELOW: Farmers' markets were–and are–at the heart of local economies throughout Texas. A chicken vendor prepares to weigh his merchandise at one such market in 1939.

BELOW, CENTER: Potatoes are one of the many important cash crops raised and sold throughout the state. Here a potato peddler naps in the back of his truck during a slow moment in 1939.

the entire state of Rhode Island. The ranch was set up in 1852. By 1854, Richard King employed so many Mexican ranch hands it is said he relocated an entire drought-stricken village to the ranch, employing the residents, who became known as "King's Men." The

ranch is still very active, maintains more than 60,000 head of cattle, and cultivates grain sorghum, cotton, sugarcane, and wildflowers. It also has banking and mercantile influence in the town of Kingsville. Many other ranches have been in continuous operation since the 1800s, and their cattle and livestock shows provide entertainment as well as business.

Of all the cash crops grown in Texas, "King Cotton" (King because of its economic domination) has been one of the most important. As early as 1745 it is recorded that several thousands of pounds

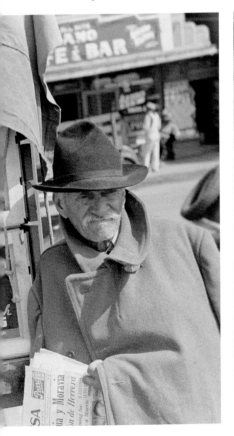

BELOW: Several men, including a delivery driver, wait at the downtown market in San Antonio in 1939. Note the large pile of fresh carrots to the left of the stone fence.

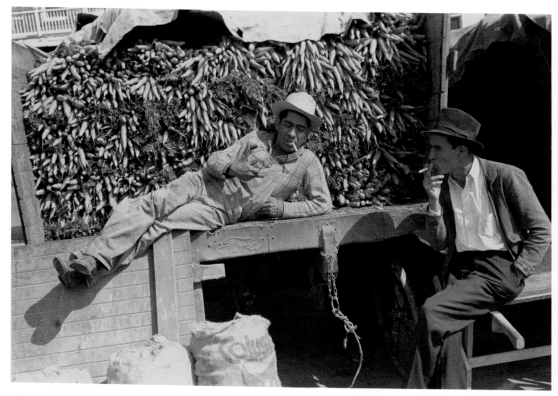

of cotton were produced annually in San Antonio. Production grew steadily, due to slave labor, sharecroppers, and tenant farmers. Cotton fibers were used for fabric, the hulls were used for cattle feed, and the seeds were crushed for cooking oil. Cotton is still raised for these purposes, as well as for ingredients in paper, fertilizer, and even tires.

Trailing not far behind is Texas's massive citrus culture. It is a bit ironic that citrus fruit wasn't indigenous to Texas. It is thought that Spaniards brought the first orange trees to Hidalgo County (near the southern tip of Texas) during the 1700s. By 1904 the first grove of commercial grapefruit trees was planted—a fruit that soon accounted for more

ABOVE: In addition to spurring important commerce, markets also provide the opportunity for a number of social contacts. This 1939 scene shows a carrot peddler and a customer discussing the events of the day over a cigarette.

ABOVE: At this farmers' market in Weatherford in 1939, a number of the men are milling about, visiting, while others sell or inspect horses. Livestock was usually sold in a different area than produce.

than two-thirds of all Texas citrus production by the 1930s. Freezes in 1949 and 1951 killed an estimated seven million (of nine million) grapefruit and orange trees, stunting that particular market for a few years. Despite disastrous freezes in 1983 and 1989, the grapefruit and orange markets are still important to Texas.

Although oil has been one of the most important businesses to Texas, it was slow to develop. Spaniards noticed oil seepage during their explorations and thought little of it, other than using it to caulk their ships and occasionally burning some for light or heat. During the nineteenth century many settlers happened upon crude, but, again, there was

a limited market for the slick black stuff. By the early 1900s, when demand for oil peaked along with the ability to find it in Texas, derricks sprang up all over in an effort to cash in on this "new" resource. Soon, oil derricks outnumbered homes and businesses in many towns. Although greatly diminished in output, the oil industry continues to add to the lore and pocketbooks of Texans.

During the Great Depression, when more than 600,000 Texans went to work for the Works Progress Administration (WPA) under Roosevelt's New Deal, schools, bridges, and many other buildings were constructed. Artists painted a total of ninety-seven murals in sixty-six post offices for "The Section of Fine

ABOVE: Of all cash crops in Texas, cotton is "King." This farmer is apparently selling cotton seed. The signs on his vehicle tout the superiority of Watson "state registered" cotton.

RIGHT: Although Texas does not produce the volume of oil it did during the early twentieth century, petroleum is still a vital part of the state's economy. Working pumps such as this one shown in 1973 in Tyler can still be found in fields and pastures.

LEFT: The University of Texas campus in Austin (shown in the 1940s) is one of the many institutions of higher learning in the state. Petroleum and rich farming and grazing lands produce the wealth to support strong educational centers.

ABOVE: Texas had a well-developed public educational system fairly early in its history. Two young children concentrate on coloring and finishing worksheets in their third-grade classroom at the Farm Security Administration camp in Weslaco in 1942.

Arts," and a surprising number still exist. The Civilian Conservation Corps (CCC) gave people work in fifteen state parks, building cabins and shelters or constructing or improving roads.

With the outbreak of World War II also came the boom in Texas shipyards, a business that really had little significance to the state before (or after) the war. However, to meet new contract deadlines, shipyards in the Orange–Port Arthur–Beaumont area, as well as those in Houston, began ramping up production in 1942. A 10,000-ton Liberty ship, the first large vessel from the Texas shipyards, was christened in April 1942. Shipyard expansion continued rapidly and brought with it numerous jobs and many small businesses. In August 1942 supplemental contracts for $200 million were received by various shipyards. By July 1943 sixty-six large ships had been launched at Houston, and production time was reduced significantly. Although there are still a few shipyards in southern Texas, most are engaged in building offshore drilling platforms and repair.

BELOW: Two men work under an oil derrick unloosening sections of pipe with giant pipe wrenches. All surfaces are covered with oil. Numerous other derricks can be seen in the background of this ca. 1939 shot taken in Kilgore.

ABOVE: A large crowd watches the auction action as stock owners bid on the grand champion bull. The important cattle industry supports fairs through the purchase of championship animals.

LEFT: Saddlery shops, found in many towns, serve the needs of those who own horses. Saddles, supplies for their care, boots, and other leather items are shown in this 1939 display window.

BELOW, FAR LEFT: A bootmaker fits the upper piece of leather to the lower one as he constructs the ubiquitous Texas cowboy boot. Boot shops are a common sight in many towns.

BELOW, LEFT: The owner of an Alpine bootmaking shop poses with a pair of boots (hanging) in 1939. This naturalized citizen from Germany found a ready market for his product in Texas.

RIGHT: The Valley Fruit Stand of Houston combined a home and business. The old house (with laundry hanging outside) has an extensive business area at street level, with bananas, grapefruit, onions, and other produce.

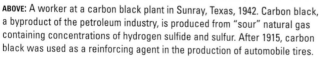

ABOVE: A worker at a carbon black plant in Sunray, Texas, 1942. Carbon black, a byproduct of the petroleum industry, is produced from "sour" natural gas containing concentrations of hydrogen sulfide and sulfur. After 1915, carbon black was used as a reinforcing agent in the production of automobile tires.

RIGHT: Texas military installations also have been an important part of the state's business and economy. A group of sailors is shown working with a PBY Catalina seaplane in Corpus Christi during World War II.

ABOVE: The town of Taylor (northeast of Austin) is known as the largest inland market for "King" cotton, which was the state's largest cash crop for many years. This sign welcomes visitors to town.

OPPOSITE: In 1939 an oil-covered worker rests for a moment on a bench. He is surrounded by giant pipe wrenches and other tools. Many other oil derricks can be seen in town behind him.

OPPOSITE, BELOW: Shown here at Club Trade Day in 1916 in Tyler, the Young Men's Business Club, apparently a forerunner to the modern Young Men's Business League, was the project of older, experienced businessmen wishing to make a difference.

RIGHT: Two cattlemen inspect a longhorn steer prior to a 2004 auction at the Fort Worth Stockyards. The historic stockyards were vital to the cattle industry through the 1960s. Volunteers now orchestrate cattle drives for the amusement of tourists.

ABOVE: Although many never received recognition, former slaves were large contributors to the success of Texas. Born a slave near San Antonio around 1850, Bob Lemmons came to Carrizo Springs during the Civil War with white cattlemen seeking new range.

RIGHT: In the 1930s, there were still quite a few surviving ex-slaves. Lou Williams was one of these. This photo forms part of "Portraits of African American ex-slaves from the U.S.," a Works Progress Administration project.

twentieth century. Eisenhower's family moved to Abilene, Kansas, two years after he was born.

Among the most flamboyant Texans is Mary Kay Ash (1918–2001), founder of Mary Kay Cosmetics and promoter of her signature pink Cadillac. After representing other companies for years, Mary Kay founded her cosmetics business in 1963, offering women homemakers one of their first real opportunities for independent income, earning commissions, jewelry, trips and—with enough sales—a pink Cadillac.

Other than Dwight D. Eisenhower (who became president), other military leaders who were Texas natives include Lt. Gen. Claire Lee Chennault (commander of the "Flying Tigers") and Adm. Chester W. Nimitz. Although not a native, Gen. John J. Pershing lived at Fort Bliss for a number of years.

In sports, the Lone Star State counts bicyclist Lance Armstrong, baseball players Ernie Banks, Roger Clemens, and Nolan Ryan, boxer George Foreman, golfers Lee Trevino and Babe Didrikson Zaharias, and gymnast Tara Lipinski as natives.

The world of news, music, and entertainment can thank Texas for Walter Cronkite, Sam Donaldson, Dan Rather,

ABOVE: Although Gen. John J. Pershing was not a native Texan, the state claims him because of his dedication and long years of residence in the state. He is shown here in 1917.

LEFT: President Dwight D. Eisenhower is frequently considered a Kansas native. However, he was born in Texas, but moved to Abilene, Kansas, when he was two years old.

BILL DRENNAN

ABOVE: Among the strong personalities from the state of Texas is Bill Drennan, a western Indian scout and sometime companion of Kit Carson.

Blind Lemon Jefferson, Buddy Holly, Bob Wills, Janis Joplin, Stevie Ray Vaughan, Selena, Willie Nelson, Roy Orbison, all three members of ZZ Top, Carol Burnett, Tommy Lee Jones, and Star Trek creator Gene Roddenberry.

Bessie Coleman, the first black woman to become a licensed aviator in the United States, was born and raised in Atlanta, Texas. She traveled the country as a stunt pilot and became the first American pilot of any race or gender to hold an international license. She died after falling out of a plane in 1926.

Other notables include Texas patriots Stephen F. Austin and Sam Houston. Both were born in Virginia, but are so instrumental to the formation and development of Texas they are claimed by the state as her own. Robert Denard (developer of DRAM—Dynamic Random Access Memory) was born in Texas, as well as Howard Hughes, Sandra Day O'Connor, H. Ross Perot, Bill Pickett (who invented rodeo "bulldog-ging"), Ann W. Richards and artist Robert Rauschenberg. Infamous Texans include Bonnie Parker and Clyde Barrow.

But one of the most intriguing of all Texas notables is Miriam "Ma" Ferguson

ABOVE: Bill Pickett (ca. 1870–1932), half African-American, half Cherokee, was the son of a slave and became the first truly well-known black rodeo cowboy. His approach to bulldogging (wrestling steers) was controversial, but his contributions remain.

LEFT: Texas patriot Sam Houston was actually born in Virginia. However, he is so closely linked with the vital history of the state, the city of Houston was named after him. Houston served as president of Texas from 1836 to 1838 and from 1841 to 1844, and was Democratic senator from the state from 1846 to 1849.

LEFT: Charles Hardin Holley (1936–1959), later known as Buddy Holly, was a lifelong resident of Texas and an early pioneer of American rock and roll. His influence extends to the Beatles, Bob Dylan, the Beach Boys, the Rolling Stones, and many others.

OPPOSITE: Elizabeth "Bessie" Coleman (1892–1926), born in Atlanta, Texas, was the first African American to become a licensed pilot and became the first American to hold an international pilot license.

OPPOSITE, FAR RIGHT: Founder of Mary Kay Cosmetics, Mary Kay Ash (1918–2001) was a lifelong Texas resident and as flamboyant as her pink Cadillacs. She once said that a company is only as good as the people it keeps.

(1875–1961). Ferguson became the first elected woman governor in the United States, when she was elected governor of Texas in 1924. She ran for office after her husband, James, had been banned from running because of corruption (he was impeached and convicted). Ma, however, was different. She openly condemned the Ku Klux Klan and issued more than 2,000 pardons to state prisoners during her first term as governor. Although defeated in the next election (in part due to her bold stance), Ferguson won the office once again in 1932. Although there were claims of bribes and cronyism, none ever stuck.

LIFE IN TEXAS

"Texas. It's a state of mind!" is a popular slogan in the Lone Star State. There is much evident in Texans' day-to-day life to support its claim. They have always been known for their fierce independence and resilience, and their history is full of corroborating evidence of these traits, from defending The Alamo to surviving the Dust Bowl years. Even the weather tests these folks, who claim to have four seasons: drought, flood, blizzard, and twister. But Texans, perhaps because of the larger-than-life nature of their state, also have had more intense highs and lows than those in many other places.

One of these high periods was during the so-called Progressive Era, roughly the 1890s through the 1920s, when the state prospered—arguably—more than most any other. An oil boom at the dawn of the twentieth century placed Texas permanently on the map of business and influence, and the growth of the combustion engine cemented the importance of "Texas tea." Population exploded, and by

"Texas does not, like any other region, simply have indigenous dishes. It proclaims them. It congratulates you, on your arrival, at having escaped from the slop pails of the other forty-nine states."

Alistair Cooke

ABOVE: Although modern residents drift by without a thought, the Brownsville Drugstore (left) dates back to 1853. It is one of many historic buildings located in Texas downtown areas.

LEFT: Surprisingly unchanged by time, the front of the Douglas Drug Store (which has housed numerous businesses) features a box-like form, decorated with simple brick dentils on a straight parapet.

LEFT: Much of village and city social life throughout Spanish-influenced Texas communities centered around the gazebo and central plaza, home to fiestas, markets, and other social gatherings.

LEFT: This theater, located in the historic section of El Paso, has undergone a number of changes characteristic of older sections of big cities. Its ornate front gives only a glimpse of life in the area a century ago.

OPPOSITE, TOP: Located along historic El Paso Street, the Colon Theatre, still in use when photographed in 1980, lies in an area inhabited since 1827 when land was given to Juan Maria Ponce de Leon. Until the 1850s, development was limited primarily to small adobe buildings.

LEFT: The El Paso Street District is the oldest, continuously used commercial area in the historic city. This building served both commercial and residential needs at the time it was photographed in 1980.

OPPOSITE, BOTTOM: Constructed in 1883 for an anticipated boom with the arrival of the railroad in 1881, the First National Bank building prospered until it failed in 1933. Several small businesses now occupy the space once taken by the bank.

1919 the state led the nation in total value of crops and cattle production. Cotton was still king as the state's primary cash crop, although red grapefruit, spinach, and other crops were strong. During this time period a large number of social, economic, political, and even moral reforms were made, including women's suffrage, Prohibition, and the direct election of senators. Spurred on by the depression of the 1890s, progressives felt the government needed to intervene more to ensure free and fair trade, and sought to expose corruption, cronyism, and monopolies. To that end, nationally, the Sherman Antitrust Act of 1890 was enacted to fight large business and unfair business practices. Texas jumped into the fray early (in part due to problems cotton farmers were having with Wall Street), becoming active in steering national policy. In 1911, a Chicago journalist made the observation that "when Texas becomes as fully developed as Ohio and Illinois, her people will control the government of the United States." Indeed, Texas soon became a major player in American politics and policy and remains so.

When the Dust Bowl era hit hard on the heels of the stock market crash of 1929, countless Texas farms and ranches literally dried up and blew away, forcing families to take to the roads in search of a better life. And when assistance came in the form of industry spurred on by World War II, Texas recovered fully. Plenty of work was found in the oil fields, in the shipbuilding yards in Galveston, Beaumont, and other cities, and help was almost always needed on farms and ranches.

LEFT: Many huge homes were built in different cities in Texas during boom times. Those that survived, such as the Marwitz House, have been used for private schools, small missions, and other outreach functions.

OPPOSITE, TOP: During the hardscrabble times of the Great Depression, many hand-to-mouth residents dreamed about homes like the Gibbs-Foster House in Grimes County–spacious but relatively simple buildings with pleasant yards.

OPPOSITE, BOTTOM LEFT: Most average Texans could only dream of owning the Abernathy-Singleton House, built in 1870 and shown here in 1966. The home exemplifies the classical architecture of northeast Texas.

OPPOSITE, BOTTOM RIGHT: This interior shot of the Abernathy-Singleton House reveals a spacious dining room (background) and large sitting room, each decorated with fine art and quality furnishings.

ABOVE: In many communities of Hispanic-dominated Texas, the church looms large in day-to-day life. The Church of Our Lady of Refuge of Sinners in Starr County (ca. 1961) represents an older style, with a cemetery in the churchyard.

Despite economic recovery and the resulting lasting prosperity in the state, Texans live in all conditions, from lavish mansions to tumbledown shacks and everything in between. But it's also not unusual—at least in the small towns—to see wealthy and poor together, visiting about the weather or arguing politics.

Day-to-day life in Texas is both very different from—and very much like—life in many other states. Urban areas are often similar to other cities, but small towns and

ABOVE: In this 1936 photo, the Church of the Divine Infant (also known as Sacred Heart) is seen in slightly hazy, diffused light.

LEFT: The "Bremond Block" in Austin, where this house is located, was a family neighborhood in itself, with six homes surrounding a common area in the center reserved for a playground for children of related families.

LEFT: Many of the old ranches in Hill Country Texas have been restored for other uses. The courtyard of this old ranch in Buda is part of the successful D.L. Jardine Salsa Company.

RIGHT: In 1939 laundry was one of the many chores of farm life. This woman is wringing freshly laundered clothes on her farm in El Indio, with her children and the hen coop in the background.

RIGHT: A barefoot young boy ambles through a small downtown business district in San Augustine in 1939, as the men of the community line the sidewalk to exchange views on various subjects.

ABOVE: A working man waits for his meal at this small-town hamburger stand (ca. 1939).

rural areas still remain the heart of Texas. Small stores and other businesses line downtown streets, people still shop locally, children still go to school and play, teenagers still hang out downtown or go to movies, and every Friday night during the fall there's Football (with a capital "F"). To Texans, these Friday night games transcend mere sports. They represent the opportunity for family and friends to gather, visit, and show unqualified support for the home team (wherever "home" is).

Religion, too, has played a major part in the life of Texans, from the early mission days through the present. Although every major religion is represented in the state, Catholics and Baptists dominate (almost two-thirds of all those who are affiliated with a religion are either Baptist or Catholic). Small chapels and churches, some very attractive, are found all over the state.

In many small towns the center of activity is still found in the town square, or plaza, whether it's a Saturday concert in the gazebo or pickups lining the street on farmers' market days. Farmers' markets in many parts of the state have always been a sight to see. Because there is such a wide variety of produce grown in Texas, the variety is tremendous—and most all of it is freshly picked. During the week (at least on truck farms), locals and immigrants can be found harvesting whatever produce is currently in season.

Texans have a lot to be proud of. They've somehow managed to preserve and nurture the deep independent spirit that allowed them to conquer such a vast area of land, while building toward a successful future for both the state and the country (although many Texans will still tell you they're an independent republic).

BELOW: A giant painted sheet metal water-melon, a "statue" commemorating the fruit's importance to the town, on display in Weatherford, a large grower of watermelons.

LEFT: In this overhead shot, a group of farmers (ca. 1939) gathers at a weekly market and examine a handbill while waiting. Note the worn car roof.

LEFT: The proprietor of an icehouse sits next to his phone in Harlingen. Once electrical cooling was possible, the ice trade became highly successful, particularly in southern Texas.

ABOVE: A soda jerk practices his trade in a small soda shop in Corpus Christi. The entertainment value of the flourish with which soda jerks made shakes was nearly worth the cost of the shake itself.

ABOVE, RIGHT: An eight-year-old newsie, 1913. During the opening years of the twentieth century, many youngsters got up early to sell papers. One ten-year-old in Waco reportedly started out at 3 a.m. each day before going to school.

RIGHT: This Dallas delivery boy for Linders Drug Store worked from 8 a.m. to 8 p.m. in 1913. The photographer, Lewis Hine, was instrumental in calling attention to child labor problems.

LEFT: Fina's Lounge, a survivor from the Guadalupe Street area of the 1950s and 1960s, is an example of the type of tiny lounges, stores, and restaurants that can be found in residential areas of larger cities.

FAR LEFT: An older candy vendor and a gentleman in a white suit have an animated conversation in front of a local café in this 1940 image from San Antonio.

LEFT: River baptisms such as this one held near Mineola, Texas, were especially popular during revivals held from the 1920s through the 1960s.

LEFT: An elderly African-American man relaxes on a bench in front of a small Corpus Christi barbecue stand that is constructed entirely of galvanized, corrugated metal.

FAR LEFT: Two men relax on the stoop of a Mexican street-side newsstand in San Antonio in 1939. Note that most of the magazines in the rack are printed in Spanish.

LEFT: The wife of a street vendor pauses for a moment of rest to have her shoes shined by a young boy while she sits in the cab of their truck.

LEFT: The owners of this general store, which opens out to the street, examine their merchandise. This store in the Mexican district of San Antonio, not uncommon for the time (1939), sold everything from garments and luggage to Mexican sombreros for tourists.

ABOVE: An outdoor street vendor sells gallon-sized cans of "Uvalde" honey (named for a small town west of San Antonio). He reads a newspaper to pass the time.

ABOVE: This San Antonio barber poses in the doorway of his shop. His wide tie and thin mustache were characteristic of the time (1939), when a haircut cost a dime.

LEFT: This group of four young men "hanging out" in front of a local clothing store. The activity wasn't much different from what older men did, but younger generations are often criticized for doing it.

BELOW, LEFT: Fastened securely to the rear of a sedan is a small chicken coop, filled with hens for sale in 1939. Note the tire and flat inner tube at left.

BELOW: This close-up full-face portrait of a farmer shows a man who has weathered the worst of the Great Depression. His appearance is likely older than his years.

LEFT: In addition to produce and stock, farmers' markets offered seeds for sale. Most every home (even non-farmers) in rural areas had a sizable garden to help sustain the family.

BELOW: In 1939 hamburgers were ten cents, cold drinks five cents, and a double-dip of ice cream was five cents at this tiny hamburger stand in Dumas. Note all the cattle brands painted around the top of the building.

ABOVE: This open-air produce market in Brownsville boasted a wide variety of fruits and vegetables, ranging from locally grown grapefruit, melons, and greens to more exotic bananas and other imported produce.

BELOW: At a large produce market in 1942, this man proudly holds up a large bundle of homegrown green onions as he smiles at the camera.

ABOVE: What does a Texas magazine vendor do when the wind kicks up? He weighs the errant publications down with pistols—a sight not seen many places today.

LEFT: A cowboy takes a break to enjoy a quick meal at a stockyards eating house in San Angelo. Note the bottle of hot sauce at left, a mainstay of the Southwest.

BELOW, LEFT: The Farm Security Administration was set up to combat rural poverty as part of the New Deal in 1935. Families of migratory workers pose in front of their row shelters at an FSA labor camp.

BELOW: A young boy builds a model airplane from scraps of wood. The two children were living at a Farm Security Administration camp with their families.

ABOVE: Even though times were tough in 1939, there was still a need to hire migrant farm workers to bring in the crops. A Mexican worker holds up a large bunch of carrots.

RIGHT: Large community clotheslines were set up at Farm Security Administration camps to accommodate the needs of multiple migrant families. Families housed at the camps ranged from displaced black and white Americans to Mexicans crossing the border to work.

LEFT: In a pose reminiscent of Millet's Sower, the wife of a Texas tenant farmer stands in an open field with a hoe. Tenant farming was a way of life for many, and is different from the more subservient life of the sharecropper.

ABOVE: Even though the Depression was beginning to let up a bit when this photo was taken in 1938, the woman was obviously living a tough life. She stated, "Do you suppose I'd be out on the highway cooking my steak if I had it good at home?"

ABOVE: A group of young boys, children of migrant workers atop a pickup truck in 1942. The middle boy (of the three sitting) is wearing an old pair of wingtip shoes with no socks.

RIGHT: A young boy (ca. 1942) sits in the middle of a cabbage crop in a small family garden plot, apparently giving credence to the legend of where children come from.

ABOVE: An aerial view of Amarillo taken in 1943 shows that while the panhandle community was already a thriving city, its outskirts gave way suddenly to flat, unbroken plains.

OPPOSITE: Four young farm boys patiently stare at the camera as the photographer records their images for posterity. The boys appear to be of different ages, common in rural classrooms.

RIGHT: This strawberry-haired, freckle-faced girl is dwarfed by the world maps mounted on the wall of her school room in San Augustine County in 1943. Geography was then considered an extremely important part of a general education.

ABOVE: Because of the shipyards and war plants, Beaumont became a boom town in 1941. The population of Jefferson County increased by 56,671 between 1941 and 1948. More than 18,000 of that number settled in the city in 1942 and 1943.

ABOVE: The 32nd Annual Conference of the National Association for the Advancement of Colored People was held in Houston, June 24–28, 1941. This partial panoramic photo shows a Boy Scout troop in the foreground.

LEFT: In 1880, the sleepy town of Burkburnett (then named Gilbert) had 132 residents. After oil was discovered there in 1912, it became a boom town, and by 1918 the town boasted a population of about 20,000.

RIGHT: The oil boom town of Burkburnett, shown here in a panoramic view, boasted nearly as many oil derricks as people. The entire downtown area is sur-rounded by hundreds of them.

RIGHT: A group of Mexican migrant workers is shown with cold drinks and candy at a service station where the truck taking them to their homes stopped in Neches, Texas.

ABOVE: Two oil field workers take time out to read the newspaper near Kilgore. While both of them are sitting on the running board, the clean man sits in the interior of the car.

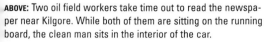

ABOVE: A group of boys plays a game of marbles in front of the FSA row houses in Robstown, Texas, while girls watch from the background.